CHECKLIST/GUIDE FOR ASSESSING DATA PROCESSING SAFEGUARDS

DEVELOPED BY
PHILLIP G. ELAM

PILOT BOOKS

Copyright © 1983 by
PILOT INDUSTRIES, INC.
103 Cooper Street, Babylon, New York, 11702
All Rights Reserved

Library of Congress Catalog Card Number: 82-22320

Library of Congress Cataloging in Publication Data

Elam, Phillip G.
    A checklist/guide for assessing data processing
safeguards.

    1. Electronic data processing departments--
Security measures. 2. Electronic data processing
departments--Safety measures. 3. Computers--Access
control. I. Title.
HF5548.2.E39 1983   658.4'78   82-22320
ISBN 0-87576-101-1

Printed in United States of America

CONTENTS

CONTENTS - CONTINUED

CONTENTS - CONTINUED

WHY THIS BOOK WAS WRITTEN

Sound management practice dictates that an organization make every reasonable effort to safeguard its assets. Data, and the computer that processes it, is as valuable as any other organizational assets. Unfortunately, it is the area that is most often overlooked and least understood.

In too many instances, management delegates the responsibility for safeguarding the data processing facility to its data processing staff. This may or may not be a sound approach, depending on the skills, knowledge, and capabilities of in-house DP personnel. For those organizations that do not have DP personnel (typical of companies using micro-computers, time-sharing services, or small business systems), the problem of protecting its DP investment may be even more critical.

This checklist provides an effective method of assessing the overall quality of procedures that have been implemented to protect the DP facility and, in the event of a disaster that would incapacitate DP, those measures that have been developed for disaster contingency planning. Presented in a "question" format, the resulting answers can help management quickly pinpoint those areas where additional safeguards are required.

1.0   PHYSICAL FACILITY CONSIDERATIONS

   1.1   Exposure to Fire Hazards

      1.1.1   Construction

         1. Is the computer housed in a building
             constructed of fire-resistant and
             noncombustible materials?

         2. Is the sub-flooring concrete or
             noncombustible with positive drainage?

         3. Is the raised flooring constructed of
             aluminum or other noncombustible material?

         4. Is the underfloor cabling channeled
             through conduits?

         5. Is the floor tiling non-petroleum based?

         6. Are the walls and trim noncombustible
             and painted with water-based fire
             retardant paints?

         7. Are doors, partitions, and framing made
             of metal?

         8. Is all glass of the steel-mesh or
             reinforced type?

         9. Is the ceiling tile made of
             noncombustible or high melting point
             materials (including supports)?

         10. Are cables connecting ceiling lighting
             placed in conduits?

         11. Are all electrical connections properly
             grounded?

         12. Has sound-deadening material (on walls,
             in cabinets, or around desks and
             operating positions) been sprayed with
             fire-retardant chemicals? (Foamed
             cellular plastics should never be used.)

         13. What is the position of the data center
             relative to sources of potential fire,
             such as cafeterias, power cabling,
             rubbish storage, caustic chemicals,
             fumes, odor, etc.?

PHYSICAL FACILITY CONSIDERATIONS (Continued)

1.1   Exposure to Fire Hazards

1.1.1   Construction

14. What is the proximity of the data center to steam lines?

15. Is the data center near areas employing hazardous processes?

16. What hazards can be removed from the immediate surrounding area?

17. Are the computer facility and the supporting facilities separated sufficiently, via proximity or fire-resistant materials, to preclude a fire in one area from affecting the other areas?

a.   Tape or disk libraries?
b.   Paper or card storage?
c.   Backup files?
d.   Source files?
e.   Source listing?
f.   Supporting operating facilities?

(1) Alternate computing facilities?

(2) Punch card processing facilities (if applicable)?

(3) Remote job entry facilities?

(4) Customer engineer facilities?

g.   Copies of operations procedures?
h.   Copies of control procedures?
i.   Forms handling equipment?
j.   Report distribution facilities?

Note: Certain facilities may be located far apart, yet be subject to inter-propagation via cable routing through vertical cable chases.

18. Are the facilities housing the activities (listed in 17) constructed of fire resistant and noncombustible material?

1.0   PHYSICAL FACILITY CONSIDERATIONS (Continued)

1.1   Exposure to Fire Hazards

1.1.1   Construction

19. If a fire were to occur in a data center facility, would other offices of the business be disabled as well?

20. Are computer room walls extended above the false ceiling to the roof?

21. Is there sufficient room between units to permit free airflow and heat dissipation?

22. Does the construction of the facilities permit distribution of detection sensors and extinguishing agents?

23. Have OSHA regulations regarding computer rooms been reviewed?

24. Are exits and fire evacuation routes clearly marked?

1.1.2   Combustibles

1. Are paper and other supplies stored outside the computer area?

2. Are curtains, rugs, furniture, and drapes noncombustible?

3. Are caustic or flammable cleaning agents permitted in the data center?

4. If flammable cleaning agents are permitted in the data center, are they kept in small quantities and in approved containers?

5. Is the quantity of combustible supplies stored in the computer room kept to the minimum?

6. Is the space beneath the access flooring used for storage of Class A materials (paper)?

7. Is sub-floor space cleaned regularly?

3

1.1   Exposure to Fire Hazards

1.1.2   Combustibles

8.   Is all furniture of metal construction?

9.   If operator documentation is kept in the computer facility, is there a backup copy stored elsewhere?

10.   Are copies of listings, tapes, disks, and card decks kept in the computer facility?

11.   Are clothing racks stored in the computer facility?

12.   Are there excess tapes, disks, or cards in the computer facility?

13.   Are report distribution and forms handling equipment kept away from the computer facility to keep dust to a minimum?

14.   Is paper bursting and shredding equipment kept away from the computer facility?

15.   Are computer room or media library safes closed when not being accessed?

16.   Are loose pieces of plastic (such as tape rings, disk covers, tape covers, empty tape reels) kept out of the computer facility?

17.   Is "decoration" of the computer room with posters, company literature, graffiti, or holiday decoration avoided?

1.1.3   Storage

1.   Are critical files "backstopped" with current copies in fireproof safes or remote facilities?

2.   Could the last several days processing be recaptured with copies of files and transactions remotely located?

1.0   <u>PHYSICAL FACILITY CONSIDERATIONS</u> (Continued)

    1.1   <u>Exposure to Fire Hazards</u>

        1.1.3   <u>Storage</u>

3. Is the number of tapes outside the tape library kept to a minimum at all times (except for remote storage)?

4. Are data safes located in a separate fire hazard area other than the tape library?

5. Is there a data safe installed in the computer room for storage of magnetic media?

6. Are disk pack storage cabinets fitted with castors to aid in emergency evacuation?

7. Are tape storage racks fitted with castors to aid in emergency evacuation?

8. Are there obstructions (risers, width of doorway, etc.) that prohibit the evacuation of storage racks?

9. Are disks and tapes containing critical files coded in their evacuation priority?

10. Are files stored in the computer room according to their evacuation priority?

11. Is there a wall in the tape library to secure tape racks and other equipment?

12. Have any existing source decks been copied to tape and stored in the data safe?

13. Are all of the user department's data files removed from the computer room?

14. Is there a data safe located in a remote area away from the computer room for backup protection?

15. Are cabinets housing card decks, tapes, or disks stored away from the computer area?

<u>PHYSICAL FACILITY CONSIDERATIONS</u> (Continued)

1.1 <u>Exposure to Fire Hazards</u>

    1.1.3   <u>Storage</u>

        16. Have alternate storage facilities been selected?

        17. In case of emergency, is transportation scheduled to move files?

        18. Have you remotely stored a supply of critical forms?

    1.1.4   <u>Practices</u>

        1. Are fire drills held regularly?

        2. Is the area under raised floors cleaned regularly?

        3. Is there adequate supply of appropriate fire fighting equipment available?

        4. Are operators trained periodically in fire fighting techniques and assigned individual responsibilities in case of fire?

        5. Is the fire detection system regularly tested?

        6. Is the no-smoking prohibition in the computer room and media library strictly enforced?

        7. Is there a documented Disaster and Security Plan?

        8. Is there an area "Fire Warden" appointed?

        9. Is the alarm system tested frequently?

        10. Are there "simulated" disasters to exercise an evacuation plan?

        11. Is a fire inspection conducted periodically by organizational or municipal fire officers?

        12. Are fire and evacuation plans easily available and reviewed periodically with the staff?

1.0   PHYSICAL FACILITY CONSIDERATIONS (Continued)

   1.1   Exposure to Fire Hazards

      1.1.4   Practices

            13.   Is the use of incendiaries controlled
                  within the facilities?

            14.   Is there a regular inspection by
                  qualified personnel of all automatic
                  detection and protection systems?

            Additional items dealing with practices are
            contained in Fire Protection and Reaction,
            and Contingency Planning.

      1.1.5   Protection and Reaction

            1.   Detection Equipment

               a.   Do the facilities have one or more
                    of the following?

                    (1)   Smoke detection equipment?*

                    (2)   Heat rise detection equipment?

                    (3)   Optical or ultra-violet
                          detection equipment?

                    (4)   Humidity control equipment?

                    (5)   Thermocoupler detectors?

                    (6)   Products of combustion
                          detectors?*

                    (7)   Air temperature detection?

               b.   Are any of these detection units
                    mounted inside the cabinets of
                    critical system components?

               c.   Are smoke detectors installed:

                    (1)   In ceiling?
                    (2)   Under raised floor?
                    (3)   In air return ducts?

               d.   Does smoke detection equipment shut
                    down the air conditioning system?

*Specifically recommended by The National Fire Protection Association
(NFPA).

1.0   PHYSICAL FACILITY CONSIDERATIONS (Continued)

    1.1   Exposure to Fire Hazards

        1.1.5   Protection and Reaction

            1.   Detection Equipment

                e.   Are smoke detectors properly
engineered to function in a
computer room?

                f.   Is the smoke detection system
tested on a scheduled basis?

                g.   Are smoke and fire detection
systems connected to the plant
security panel and municipal police
departments?

                h.   Does the smoke detection system
have any electrical count-down time
(180 to 0 seconds)?

                i.   Are under-floor smoke detector
heads identified by hanging markers
in the computer room ceiling?

            2.   Alarm Mechanisms

                a.   Do the facilities listed above
provide alarm mechanisms, such as
automatic alarming upon detection
of fire (light), smoke, or
inordinate heat rise?

                b.   Are there several strategically
located manually-operated alarm
systems?

                c.   Does the alarm device report the
location of the fire to a
centralized or municipal fire or
security position?

                d.   Does the alarm system provide a
pre-alarm audible tone?

                e.   Does the alarming mechanisms
contain automatic shut down of
critical equipment? (Particularly
required with sprinkler systems.)

1.0   PHYSICAL FACILITY CONSIDERATIONS (Continued)

   1.1   Exposure to Fire Hazards

      1.1.5   Protection and Reaction

         2.   Alarm Mechanisms

            f.   Is there a smoke detector alarm
                 horn in a central location in the
                 computer room?

            g.   Does the alarm sound:

               (1)   Locally?
               (2)   At watchman's station?
               (3)   At central station?
               (4)   At fire or police headquarters?

         3.   Protection Equipment

            Do the facilities have one or more of
            the following?

            a.   Automatic dispersal of fire
                 extinguishing or retardant agent,
                 such as:

               (1)   Gas--Halon 1301 (above and
                     beneath floors and ceilings)?
                     Have personnel been trained
                     both in the use of the gas and
                     personal safety measures?

               (2)   Foam?

               (3)   Water (last resort), including
                     hoses and/or sprinkling
                     systems?

                  a)   Wet pipe (releases water
                       at a set temperature)?

                  b)   Pre-action (may sound an
                       alarm and delay release
                       of water)?

               (4)   Fixed flooding systems?

               (5)   Dry suppressants?

1.0   PHYSICAL FACILITY CONSIDERATIONS (Continued)

    1.1 Exposure to Fire Hazards

        1.1.5   Protection and Reaction

           3.   Protection Equipment

              b.   Manual Equipment, such as:

(1) Portable extinguishers for electrical and other fires?

(2) Are portable fire extinguishers located strategically around the area with location markers clearly visible over computer equipment?

(3) Water or other extinguishing agent for nonelectrical fires?

(4) Are these located throughout the facilities where they can be easily obtained within a few steps?

(c) Automatic and/or delayed interruption of power sources where electrical fires have been discovered?

(d) Automatic shutdown of air conditioning systems (particularly where Halon 1301 is used)?

(e) Automatic shutdown of heating or humidity systems?

(f) Automatic close-off of air ducts?

(g) Automatic illumination of emergency lighting due to interruption of the prime power source?

(h) Automatic sealing of fire-breaks or fire-doors between sections of the facility?

(i) Are there any fire suppressant outlets mounted inside the cabinets of critical system components?

1.0   PHYSICAL FACILITY CONSIDERATIONS (Continued)

1.1   Exposure to Fire Hazards

1.1.5   Protection and Reaction

3.   Protection Equipment

(j)   Is there a means to activate an automatic system manually?

(k)   Are automatic devices "rate-compensated" to allow for sudden increases in temperature?

(l)   Does emergency power shutdown include the air conditioning system?

4.   Reaction Planning

a.   Have building engineers analyzed the fire detection system to ensure that the number and location of detectors are appropriate for the current configuration?

b.   Is the local fire fighting force rated in accordance with the American Insurance Association's Standard Fire Defense Rating Schedule?

c.   Is there around-the-clock watchman coverage during nonworking hours?

d.   What procedures exist to "re-arm" any fire-protection equipment?

e.   Does the construction of the facilities permit easy access by fire-fighting personnel and equipment?

f.   Can emergency crews gain access to the installation without delay?

g.   If access is through an electrically controlled system, can it be operated by standby battery power?

h.   Are emergency power shutdown controls easily accessible at points of exit?

11

1.0   PHYSICAL FACILITY CONSIDERATIONS (Continued)

    1.1 Exposure to Fire Hazards

        1.1.5   Protection and Reaction

            4.   Reaction Planning

                i.   Can emergency crews gain access to the computer room without excess delay during off-shifts and holidays?

                j.   Is self-contained breathing apparatus available to fire-fighting personnel?

                k.   Are additional floor panel removers installed adjacent to fire extinguishers?

                l.   Have locations been identified and personnel informed of the sprinkler shut-off valve for annexes, computer operations and data entry?

                m.   Does the fire department know the location of both the computer room and alarm devices? Is there a reception area that contains indicators of alarm conditions in the computer facility?

                n.   Is there a battery powered megaphone available and are personnel knowledgeable of its location and operation?

    1.2 Water Hazard/Damage Exposure

        1.2.1   Physical Location

            1.   Are computers excluded from areas below grade?

            2.   If not, have sufficient sealing and foundation draining devices been included?

1.2   Water Hazard/Damage Exposure

    1.2.2   Intra-Facility

1. Are overhead steam or water pipes (except sprinklers) eliminated?

2. Is there drainage under the raised floor sufficient to remove accumulated liquid quickly?

3. Are drains installed on floor above to divert accumulated water from all hardware?

4. Is the upper ceiling constructed so as to conduct water from higher levels away from the computer facility?

5. Is the floor above watertight?

6. Are the pipe and wire openings watertight?

7. Is there adequate drainage to prevent water overflow from adjacent areas?

8. In an industrial-type vacuum cleaner (that will pick up water) readily available to the computer facility?

9. Is there a dispenser for a roll of plastic to be used for covering the hardware in the event the sprinkler heads discharge?

10. Are all electrical junction boxes under the raised flooring held off the slab to prevent water damage?

11. Are there sufficient ducts to conduct water used in air conditioning systems away from the building?

12. Is there a dry well in a ground floor facility?

1.0   <u>PHYSICAL FACILITY CONSIDERATIONS</u> (Continued)

   1.2   <u>Water Hazard/Damage Exposure</u>

      1.2.3   <u>Outside The Facility</u>

         1.   Is the roof sufficiently sealed to prevent opening and subsequent leakage caused by wind damage?

         2.   Is there protection against accumulated air conditioning water or leaks in rooftop water towers?

         3.   Are exterior windows and doors watertight?

         4.   Is grading around the exterior of the facility constructed to conduct water away from the building?

         5.   Are there sufficient storm drain inlets to accommodate water accumulation during sudden or seasonal rainfall?

         6.   Have subterranean or under-roofing heating systems been installed to melt snow?

   1.3   <u>Air Conditioning Considerations</u>

      1.3.1   <u>Air Conditioning Facility</u>

         1.   Are the BTU ratings of air conditioning equipment appropriate for the facility?

         2.   Is the air conditioning system used exclusively for the computer area?

         3.   Is there a backup air conditioning capability?

         4.   Is the compressor remote from the computer room?

         5.   Has the air conditioning equipment been placed in a high place with restricted access?

      1.3.2   <u>Intakes, Ducting, and Piping</u>

         1.   Are duct linings and filters noncombustible?

14

1.3 Air Conditioning Considerations

    1.3.2   Intakes, Ducting, and Piping

        2. Are air intakes:

            a. Covered with protective screening?

            b. Located well above street level?

            c. Located so as to prevent intake of pollutants or other debris?

        3. Could ducting carry fumes and smoke to other offices?

    1.3.3   Shutdown

        1. Will alarm or sensing devices automatically shut down the air conditioning system?

        2. Are there alternate locations in the computer room area where all power and air conditioning fans for the area can be shut off?

        3. Can installed ceiling exhaust fan(s) provide sufficient air movement if the air conditioning system is inoperable for several hours?

    1.3.4   Protection

        1. Is the cooling tower fire-protected?

        2. Are there sensors installed within the air conditioning system?

        3. Does the construction of the air conditioning facilities permit only authorized access, including:

            a. Placement in a high place to restrict access?

            b. Protection of the source of water supply?

            c. Protection of fan or cooling mechanisms?

1.3   Air Conditioning Considerations

1.3.4   Protection

d.   Survey of air conditioning area by closed circuit television?

e.   Periodic check by security personnel?

4.   Do security personnel have copies of wiring, ducting, water, and air flow diagrams for use by maintenance or fire fighting personnel?

5.   Is there heat or humidity control equipment?

6.   Are there temperature and humidity monitoring and recording devices?

1.4   Electrical Considerations

1.4.1   Power Supply

1.   Is the local electrical power reliable?

a.   Is there sufficient voltage and amperage to support the equipment when it is all operating?

b.   How susceptible is this power supply to:

(1)   Outages?
(2)   Reduced operating voltages?
(3)   Surges of power "spikes"?

c.   If electrical power is unreliable, have alternate power sources been investigated?

(1)   Secondary sources?
(2)   Standby generators?
(3)   Uninterruptible Power Source (UPS)?

d.   Is the voltage input monitored with a recording voltmeter that displays changes?

1.4   Electrical Considerations

1.4.1   Power Supply

2.   Does the data center have a devoted power system? (The source of power should not connect to other parts of the organization.)

3.   Is there an alternate power source that permits resumption of operation if the prime power source is destroyed?

4.   Are the computer room transformer and motor generator enclosed in a wire cage for protection?

5.   Is there standby battery power to operate electrically controlled doors during power failures?

1.4.2   Wiring

1.   Is wiring in conformance with local building codes for the installation's class of service?

2.   Do security and maintenance officials have a copy of the wiring diagram?

3.   Are electrical boxes placed in areas not exposed to water or other damage?

4.   Are the main power control boards in a remote or restricted access position?

5.   Are there emergency power-off switches at each exit of the computer room to meet OSHA requirements?

6.   Has all wiring under the raised floor in the computer room been checked, assuring that all circuits, including 110V, are wired to breakers and properly grounded?

1.4.3   Lighting

1.   Is there an emergency lighting system which activates when the main lighting fails?

1.0   PHYSICAL FACILITY CONSIDERATIONS (Continued)

   1.4 Electrical Considerations

      1.4.3   Lighting

         2.   If there is an emergency lighting
              system, has it been recently tested?

         3.   If the system has fixed-position lamps,
              have they been tested to see if they
              illuminate the proper area?

         4.   Are there sources of light,
              strategically located, that do not
              depend upon the main power source?

         5.   Is there an emergency power source to
              energize emergency lighting?

         6.   Are the office lights wired to provide a
              security night light?

         7.   Have emergency lights for the computer
              room, annex, and data entry area been
              installed?

         8.   Has a copy of the layout been given to
              the Maintenance Department?

   1.5 Preparing for Civil, Man-Made, and Natural Disasters

      1.5.1   Location

         1.   Is the facility remote from any
              earthquake fault?

         2.   Is the facility located in a river bed
              or flood plain?

         3.   Is the facility close to high voltage
              transmission lines?

         4.   Is the facility close to heavily
              traveled highways?

         5.   Is the facility close to rail lines?

         6.   Is the facility close to fuel storage
              containers?

         7.   Is the facility close to fuel
              transmission lines?

18

1.5   Preparing for Civil, Man-Made, and Natural Disasters

1.5.1   Location

8. Is the facility close to isolated metal structures that might draw lightning?

9. Is the facility located in a high crime area?

10. Have there been reports of local civil unrest, vis-a-vis computer facilities?

11. Is the facility in an area of high fire potential?

12. Is the facility close to an airport?

13. Is the facility close to steam transmission lines?

14. Is the facility close to the storage of toxic or caustic chemicals?

15. Is the facility located in an area of dense trees or other tall foliage?

16. Is the facility located in an area where flora is allowed to dry, ripen, or compost?

17. Would disasters occurring in adjacent structures have a deleterious effect on your facility?

18. Is the facility located where problems with small animals and/or rodents might be a problem?

1.5.2   Construction

1. Is the building structurally sound:

   a. To resist wind storms and hurricanes?

   b. To resist flood damage?

   c. To resist earthquakes?

1.0   <u>PHYSICAL FACILITY CONSIDERATIONS</u> (Continued)

1.5   <u>Preparing for Civil, Man-Made, and Natural Disasters</u>

1.5.2   <u>Construction</u>

2.   Are buildings and equipment properly grounded for lightning protection?

3.   Is the building on a solid foundation?

4.   Is the building constructed so as to be "defensible" in the case of civil unrest?

5.   Is the building constructed to permit access to emergency crews and equipment?

1.5.3   <u>Natural Disaster Prediction</u>

1.   Is there some means to advise personnel of possible natural disaster, such as:

a.   Rain or snow?

b.   Tornado, hurricane, or high winds?

c.   Severe electrical disturbance?

d.   Sand storms?

e.   Rising rivers?

2.   Is there a series of contingency steps that are invoked when a natural disaster advisory is received? If not, why not?

1.5.4   <u>Man-Made Disaster Prediction</u>

1.   Will appropriate personnel be notified in the case of a nearby disaster, such as fire in adjacent buildings?

2.   If the facility is in the flight path of an airport, will it be notified of potential aircraft difficulty?

1.5.5   <u>Civil Disaster Prediction</u>

1.   Is someone appointed to "keep tabs" on the potential unrest in the locale?

1.0   PHYSICAL FACILITY CONSIDERATIONS (Continued)

   1.5   Preparing for Civil, Man-Made, and Natural Disasters

      1.5.5   Civil Disaster Prediction

         2.   Is there a procedure for civil
               authorities to notify the facility in
               the event of civil unrest?

         3.   Does the company's contract with any
               security services agency provide for
               "profiling any potential unrest?"

         4.   Is there a policy for threat monitoring?

         5.   Is there a policy for handling and
               controlling rumors?

         6.   What arrangements exist?

   1.6   Alternate Location Considerations

      1.   Is there an alternate location for resumption of
            operations following a disaster?

      2.   Is space allotted for:

         a.   Computer hardware?

         b.   Forms handling and distribution equipment?

         c.   Data preparation?

         d.   Documentation files?

         e.   Program files?

         f.   Tape files? Disk files?

         g.   Programming functions?

         h.   Administrative functions?

         i.   Supply storage?

         j.   Air conditioning and electrical equipment?

<u>PHYSICAL FACILITY CONSIDERATIONS</u> (Continued)

1.6 <u>Alternate Location Considerations</u>

3. Is there an alternate site implementation plan?

   a. Has it been approved by facilities personnel?

   b. Has it been approved by security personnel?

   c. Has it been coordinated with key users?

4. Are there arrangements for both transportation or equipment and other service considerations?

5. Is there need for stocking the alternate facility with food, shelter, or supply items?

1.7 <u>Access Control Considerations</u>

1.7.1 <u>Identification</u>

1. Is advertising the location of the computer facility discouraged?

2. Is access to the computer area restricted to selected personnel?

3. Is there a photo badge system for positive identification of employees?

4. What mechanisms exist to ensure that the person is carrying his/her own badge?

5. Does data center have a current photograph of every person with legitimate access to the area?

6. Is a person admitted merely because he/she is known?

7. Is a person admitted merely because he/she is accompanied by a known person?

8. In the case of temporary badges, is the badge matched against some other form of identification?

9. Are identification badges color-coded, facility-zoned, or in some other means marked to demonstrate security clearance or access?

1.7   Access Control Considerations

1.7.1   Identification

10.   Are transient personnel checked out of, as well as into the computer room?

11.   Can just anybody ask for and receive data files or reports?

12.   If not, is there a procedure to ensure:

   a.   Security clearance or the individual relative to the files or reports sought?

   b.   The "need to know" access permitted relative to the files or reports sought?

13.   Are all visitors challenged?

14.   Are people free to carry anything in and out of the facility?

15.   Are food and beverages prohibited in the computer room?

1.7.2   Access Routes

1.   Are there guards on all street entrances that lead to the computer area?

2.   Do elevator doors open on the data center floor near the data center?

3.   Do hallways have false floors that could permit unauthorized access to the computer room?

4.   Are accesses from stairways restricted or in any way controlled?

5.   Are access routes to and from nearby offices controlled?

6.   Are all exterior windows at or near street level covered with expanded metal grills?

1.7   Access Control Considerations

1.7.2   Access Routes

7. In areas with a high crime rate, is there bullet-proof glass or are windows taped for entry detection?

8. Is there a "dumb waiter" or freight elevator that could be used as an unauthorized access route?

9. Is access controlled from a loading dock?

10. If the facilities have electrically operated doors, can they be opened manually if the power source is interrupted to gain unauthorized access?

11. Is the computer room screened so that it is not visible from the street?

12. If not, could access be gained through street level windows?

13. Are the doors to the computer room and annex locked during second shift, third shift, and weekends?

1.7.3   Visitor Control

1. Are personnel trained to challenge improperly identified visitors?

2. Is there a visitor control procedure?

3. Is there a computer room sign in/out log for visitors?

4. Are temporary passes numbered to permit control of the pass, as well as the person using it?

5. Is there a procedure for returning and accounting for temporary passes?

6. Can temporary passes be duplicated easily?

7. Are pass and access rules consistently enforced?

1.7 Access Control Considerations

1.7.3   Visitor Control

8. Can anyone who wants to see the data center do so on request?

9. Are vendor personnel allowed to "roam freely" because of their apparent vendor affiliation?

10. Is the casual visitor eliminated by stopping organization executives from including the data center in a facilities tour?

11. Does someone accompany all visitors?

12. Are visitors excluded from sensitive areas of the facility?

13. Are visitors controlled under the suggestions for access contained in these guidelines?

14. Where sensitive data or files are concerned, is there positive security clearance for the visitor?

1.7.4   Security

1. Is access to the computer or other related facilities controlled?

2. Are keys, cipher locks, and other security devices utilized to control access?

3. Can a single individual be prevented from gaining access during off-shift hours without the knowledge of a security guard or another employee?

4. Is there around-the-clock watchman service?

5. Has closed circuit television equipment been installed:

   a. To cover critical equipment?

1.7 Access Control Considerations

    1.7.4   Security

        b.   To cover access routes?

        c.   To cover critical data storage locations?

        d.   To cover air conditioning and power sources?

        e.   Beneath false floors and above false ceilings?

        f.   To cover critical communications equipment and devices?

        g.   To permit monitoring by safety or security officials?

        h.   On the outside of entrances and building periphery?

6.   Are hallways covered by closed circuit television?

7.   Is it possible for someone to access communications lines externally?

8.   Have identification markings been removed from power rooms, communications closets, etc.?

9.   Is access to communications equipment, such as junction boxes, switching mechanisms, terminal outlets, etc., freely available?

10. Are there restrictions on the introduction of camera or other photo recording equipment in the data center?

11. Are there restrictions on the introduction of sound magnetic recording equipment, radios or other electronic devices in the data center area?

12. Is metal detection equipment available? Is it used?

1.7   Access Control Considerations

    1.7.4   Security

13. Is there a means to inspect parcels and other articles moved in and out of the data center?

14. What guarantee is there that boxes or crates containing products or equipment received at the data center actually contained their specified contents?

15. Are there "alert" mechanisms for the summoning of security personnel?

16. Are there electric eye or proximity warning indicators positioned in infrequently used rooms or hallways?

17. Have self-closing mechanisms been installed on all internal doors?

18. Are internal doors and passageways free of all obstructions, including wedges?

19. Are internal aisles wide, straight, and free of obstructions?

20. Is all equipment positioned so that access doors open fully and freely?

21. Once open, do cabinet doors permit room for a person to work on the device?

22. Are there magnetic sensors in access doorways?

23. Are there security guards at all data center accesses?

24. Are critical files "under lock and key," limiting the access?

25. Is there a periodic security check of all personnel?

    a.   Spot inspection under operation?

    b.   Complete background investigation before hiring?

1.0 PHYSICAL FACILITY CONSIDERATIONS (Continued)

1.0   PHYSICAL FACILITY CONSIDERATIONS (Continued)

   1.7 Access Control Considerations

      1.7.4   Security

               c.   Thorough investigation of all
                    personnel with access to the data
                    center?

           26. In addition to closed circuit
                television, are there sound monitoring
                systems that permit security personnel
                to "listen in" while the facilities are
                unused?

           27. Can all external doors be locked on
                command?

           28. If there is a closed circuit television,
                has someone been assigned to watch the
                monitors at all times?

           29. Are there double door arrangements that
                will "lock-in" an intruder between them?

           30. Are the security precautions the same at
                every entrance, including the loading
                dock?

           31. Are plans and blueprints for the data
                center and other important areas
                controlled or restricted? Where are they
                available outside the organization?

           32. Are there external walls and windows
                that permit easy access for a
                saboteur?

           33. If the organization is subject to a
                civil disturbance, is the disaster plan
                filed with local police, fire, civil
                defense, and/or National Guard officials?

           34. Are master controls for detection and
                suppression systems located outside the
                data center?

           35. Are communications devices and equipment
                relative to the data center in a remote
                or restricted access area?

           36. Is there a procedure for access control?

1.7   Access Control Considerations

1.7.4   Security

37. Are monitoring devices connected to access doors, emergency exits, and windows for the computer room and annex, connected to company security system?

38. Are master key locks removed from the exterior of emergency exits?

39. Are file areas segregated so that only specific individuals have access to them?

40. Are plexi-glass windows installed between the data entry area and the computer room and between the computer room annex and computer room to reduce the personnel traffic?

41. Is a badge reader access control system installed for the computer room and the computer room annex?

42. Are data safe combinations changed upon termination of any employee knowing the combination?

43. Do watchmen or other security officials perform an inspection of the facilities at regular intervals when not in use?

1.7.5   Procedures

1. Does only authorized personnel have access to the computer facility and to programs, data, documentation, and procedures?

2. Is there a system of signatures to control access to critical data and documents?

3. Is there a control sheet to cross reference console log number to CPU hours by shift?

4. Are there updates to all completed and planned security/physical changes?

1.0   PHYSICAL FACILITY CONSIDERATIONS (Continued)

    1.7   Access Control Considerations

        1.7.5   Procedures

            5.   Are there quarterly departmental review meetings on security and control procedures?

            6.   Is there a periodic review of the scope of confidential reporting to include order processing, billing, and data control procedures?

            7.   Have you reviewed with the organization's messengers/mail room the handling steps for incoming/outgoing confidential mail and reports?

            8.   Are there established procedures to periodically require all individuals authorized to receive reports to show possession of badge access cards?

            9.   Are confidential reports distributed by use of interoffice mailing envelopes? Report distribution should be labeled with a code designating mailing method.

    1.8   Housekeeping

        1.   Is there an accumulation of trash in the computer area?

        2.   Are equipment covers and work surfaces cleaned regularly?

        3.   Are floors washed regularly?

        4.   Are wastebaskets emptied outside the computer area to reduce dust discharge?

        5.   Is carpeting of the anti-static type?

        6.   Is eating discouraged in the computer room?

        7.   Are low fire hazard waste containers used?

        8.   Is smoking allowed in the computer room? If so, are self-extinguishing ash trays used?

        9.   Are maintenance areas kept clean and orderly?

1.0   PHYSICAL FACILITY CONSIDERATIONS (Continued)

   1.8 Housekeeping

      10. Are all areas vacuumed underneath the raised floor
           of the computer room?

      11. Is there a mandated and enforced housekeeping
           procedure that ensures that flammable materials
           (such as paper, inks, corrugated boxes, and
           ribbons) are kept to a minimum?

      12. Are closed circuit TV lenses cleaned regularly?

   1.9 Other Facility Considerations

      1.   Are security and operations personnel briefed on
           how to react to civil disturbances?

      2.   Is there a good liaison program with local law
           enforcement agencies?

      3.   Do personnel know how to handle telephone bomb
           threats?

      4.   Is glass removed from computer room walls and
           replaced with aluminum panels (in a civil
           disturbance)?

      5.   Are report distribution systems installed in any
           annex and removed from the computer room?

      6.   Are all signs indicating the location of the
           computer room and any computer room annex removed?

      7.   Are intercom systems installed between computer
           room and other departments?

      8.   Are there dry cell lanterns available for computer
           room emergency use?

      9.   Are door hinges on all doors to the computer room
           and computer room annex welded?

      10. Is there a paper shredder to destroy confidential
           reports?

      11. Are there metal trash receptacles with hinged
           covers?

1.0   <u>PHYSICAL FACILITY CONSIDERATIONS</u> (Continued)

    1.9 <u>Other Facility Considerations</u>

        12. Have locks been installed on the windows
             connecting the data entry area and computer
             operations?

        13. What is the proximity of the data center to the
             organization's medical facilities?

2.0   PERSONNEL

2.1 Selection and Evaluation

1.   Are background checks performed on all newly-hired employees?

   a.   Security check?

   b.   Psychological testing?

   c.   Complete reference check?

   d.   Attitude profile?

2.   Are employees rechecked periodically?

   a.   Security?

   b.   Performance evaluation?

   c.   Attitude profile?

3.   Are supervisors alert to the possibility of a disgruntled employee?

   a.   Conflict between employees?

   b.   Dissatisfaction over pay, company policies, or other company-related incidents, such as working conditions, work period, or performance evaluation?

   c.   Possible personal problems with family, finances, etc.?

4.   Do personnel policies allow for containment or immediate dismissal of employees who may constitute a threat to the installation?

   a.   Notification procedures?

   b.   Minority considerations?

   c.   Political considerations?

2.0   <u>PERSONNEL</u> (Continued)

    2.1 <u>Selection and Evaluation</u>

        5. Do supervisors know their people well enough to detect a change in their living habits?

           a. Financial status?

           b. Living conditions?

           c. Clothing, automobile, etc.?

    2.2 <u>Training and Operating Procedures</u>

        2.2.1   <u>Training Orientation</u>

           1. Is there a continuing personnel education program in computer security?

           2. Are the personnel trained for an orderly shutdown of the equipment for various types of emergencies, such as fire, earthquake, and bomb threat?

           3. Are there orientation sessions dealing with emergency procedures?

           4. Has a fire extinguisher demonstration been held for all operators?

           5. Have computer operators attended a class on computer room security?

        2.2.2   <u>Functional Procedures</u>

           1. Are procedures strategically located and prominently displayed for:

             a. Extinguishing agents?

             b. Emergency telephone numbers:

                (1) Fire?
                (2) Police?
                (3) Ambulance?
                (4) Security?

             c. Direct line telephone handsets?

             d. Evacuation plans?

             e. Responsibility assignments?

2.2 Training and Operating Procedures

2.2.2   Functional Procedures

f.   First aid equipment and supplies?

g.   Exit routes (arrows or colored lines on the floor) and lighted exit signs?

2   Have the involved people read and understood these procedures?

3.   Is there a periodic review of these procedures with the involved people?

4.   Are new employees familiar with these procedures as part of their initiation to the organization?

5.   Is there a specific plan for fire drills?

6.   Are periodic fire drills conducted to test and improve the plan?

7.   Are key personnel, at the minimum, trained in first-aid procedures to treat burns and smoke inhalation (such as hydrogen chloride gas from insulation)? How about CPR?

8.   Is there first aid equipment available within the facilities and do key personnel know its location, contents, and use?

9.   Have all personnel been trained in the use of fire fighting equipment?

10.   Is the location of additional equipment for such use known to all personnel?

11.   Are people cross-trained to cover all functions?

a.   Can more than one operator on each shift operate each piece of hardware?

b.   Can more than one operator on each shift run each system?

35

2.0   PERSONNEL (Continued)

   2.2   Training and Operating Procedures

      2.2.2   Functional Procedures

         c.   Can more than one person on each
               shift perform each emergency task?

         d.   Does each person have a primary and
               secondary emergency assignment?

      12.   Is processing of all confidential work
             restricted to specific operators?

      13.   Are operators scheduled on rotation
             basis for console and I/O on all shifts?

      2.2.3   Emergency Work Assignments and Procedures

      1.   Do the personnel have assigned duties in
            case of fire?

         a.   Who will power-down the equipment?

         b.   Who will remove critical data files?

         c.   Who will attempt short-term fire
               fighting measures?

         d.   Who will oversee evacuation
               measures?

         e.   Who will notify fire or other
               responsible officials?

         f.   Who will "cut" the power?

         g.   Who will turn off the air
               conditioning?

         h.   Who will have the responsibility to
               attend to injured personnel?

      2.   Are evacuation procedures assigned to
            each staff member or zone within the
            facility?

2.0   <u>PERSONNEL</u> (Continued)

    2.2   <u>Training and Operating Procedures</u>

        2.2.3   <u>Emergency Work Assignments and Procedures</u>

            3.   Are there specific procedures for equipment use in the case of fire, such as power-down procedures to prevent destruction of critical data and devices?

                a.   Does each employee have a copy?

                b.   Is there a copy prominently displayed?

                c.   Do security officials have a copy?

                d.   Do fire officials have a copy?

            4.   If automated systems do not function because of a disaster, are there up-to-date manual backup systems that will permit the organization to continue operation?

            5.   Would the backup systems or procedures permit the organization to cover its short-term needs?

            6.   Has a person been designated to review the items contained in this checklist?

            7.   Does this person have the authority to affect changes or to convince funding authorities to underwrite necessary improvements?

            8.   Do insurance, safety, and fire prevention officials periodically review procedures drawn from this checklist?

2.0   PERSONNEL (Continued)

2.2   Training and Operating Procedures

2.2.3   Emergency Work Assignments and Procedures

9.   Are there people who conduct a weekly
security check?

10. Must personnel use prenumbered console
log sheets that are retained after daily
use?

11. Is there a periodic inspection to
identify needed improvements?

2.3   Service Personnel

2.3.1   In-House

1.   Is access to vital areas controlled for
custodial, electrical, and other
in-house maintenance personnel?

2.   Must a computer center employee be
present when such individuals are in the
area?

2.3.2   Vendor

1.   Are there a list of each vendor's
authorized service and systems support
personnel?

2.   Must vendor personnel supply positive
identification?

3.   Are their activities supervised to assure
that they do not compromise security?

4.   Must vendors verify that they have
performed a background check on their
personnel?

2.3.3   Other

1.   How are "casual" people (such as
maintenance and repair personnel from
outside the organization) evaluated?

3.0   SECURITY

3.1 Hardware Security Considerations

    3.1.1   Physical Security

        1.   Have the access and location requirements of these guidelines been met?

        2.   Has remotely located hardware (such as data entry terminals, display units, printers, card readers, communications equipment, etc.) received the access and location protection detailed in these guidelines?

    3.1.2   Logical Security

        1.   Are "forms" displayed on screens indefinitely for someone to determine the contents of accessed data files?

        2.   Is there a means to block or distort access codes and passwords entered to the system?

    3.1.3   Utilization

        1.   Are all operations monitored for compliance with schedules?

        2.   Has an acceptable range of times for transactions handling been established?

        3.   Are meter hours correlated with utilization hours?

        4.   Has an acceptable range of correlation of meter versus utilization hours been established?

        5.   Do employees have access to tools with which they might do harm or "experiment" with the hardware?

        6.   Are scheduled maintenance activities monitored to assure proper reliability and hardware performance?

        7.   Is there a mechanism to verify that maintenance claimed is maintenance performed?

3.0   <u>SECURITY</u> (Continued)

   3.1   <u>Hardware Security Considerations</u>

      3.1.3   <u>Utilization</u>

            8.   Have record systems, indicating vendors,
                 model numbers, features, and level of
                 engineering change been established?

            9.   Are all periods of down-time verified?

            10. Does each period of down-time have a
                 corresponding maintenance log?

            11. Is "end meter" checked with "begin
                 meter" readings each morning for
                 unexplained gaps?

            12. Are steps taken to resolve unexplained
                 time periods?

            13. Is all incoming work checked against an
                 authorized user list?

            14. Is output spot-checked for possible
                 misuse of the system?

            15. Is there an updated distribution system
                 to prevent an unauthorized person from
                 receiving a confidential report?

      3.1.4   <u>Backup</u>

            1.   Are arrangements made for backup
                 computer service in the same or
                 another facility?

            2.   If there are backup arrangements, has
                 the system to be backed-up been run with
                 that hardware to ensure compatibility?

            3.   Is time available at the backup site
                 sufficient to absorb the backup work?

            4.   If the backup site can accommodate the
                 load, could it do so for the days,
                 weeks, or months necessary to get the
                 system functioning again?

3.0   <u>SECURITY</u> (Continued)

    3.1   <u>Hardware Security Considerations</u>

        3.1.5   <u>Tapes and/or Disks</u>

1. Is there a procedure for tape and/or disk accountability?

2. Does the tape and disk accountability procedure cover:

   a. Frequency of use?

   b. Frequency of cleaning?

   c. Authorized user?

   d. Security classification?

   e. External evacuation classification?

   f. Release procedures?

3. Are magnetic tapes and disks filed in an orderly manner?

4. Is there a tape and/or disk cleaning plan?

   a. Are tapes cleaned on a regular basis?

5. Are tapes kept in their containers except when being used?

6. Are tapes stored vertically?

7. Are tape utilization records maintained?

8. Are tape containers cleaned periodically?

9. Are tape heads cleaned every shift?

10. Are tapes sample tested periodically for drop-outs, to determine the general condition of the tape library?

11. Is frayed leader stripped regularly?

12. Has the possibility of a tape rehabilitation or recertification program been investigated?

41

3.0   SECURITY (Continued)

    3.1   Hardware Security Considerations

        3.1.5   Tapes and/or Disks

            13.   Is the tape library located in an area not subject to explosion or other dangers?

            14.   Are storage vaults specifically designed for magnetic media used for critical tape files?

            15.   Has magnetic detection equipment been considered to preclude the presence of a magnet near tapes and disks?

            16.   Is similar protection provided for tape files while in transit to a backup site, etc.

    3.2   Software Security Considerations

        3.2.1   Physical Security

            1.   Are essential programs, software systems, and associated documentation in the program library located in a locked vault or secured area?

            2.   Have you provided backup files at a secondary location for programs and associated documentation?

            3.   Are all copies of pertinent software treated in the same manner of control?

            4.   In the event that physical security is compromised, is the company legally protected or insured against the compromise?

            5.   If the software is compromised, can replacement software be obtained immediately?

3.0   <u>SECURITY</u> (Continued)

3.2   <u>Software Security Considerations</u>

3.2.2   <u>Access Restrictions</u>

1.   Is access to the essential programs and
        software systems on a need-to-know basis
        in prime and backup areas?

        a.   Has it been determined who is to
                have access to various parts of the
                software?

        b.   Is there a signatory procedure for
                obtaining copies of critical
                software?

2.   Is a multi-level access control to data
        files used?

        a.   By various levels of security
                classification?

        a.   By various breakdowns within a
                file; that is, by block, record,
                field, characters?

        c.   By read-only, write-only, update,
                etc.?

3.   Are periodic checks made to validate the
        security software utilities and tables
        of access codes?

4.   If remote access to on-line data bases
        is used, are there techniques to prevent
        more than one user from updating files
        at any given time?

3.2.3   <u>Remote Terminals</u>

1.   Is keyword or password protection used?

        a.   If so, are keywords and passwords
                changed often?

        b.   Is the use of easily discernable or
                "cute" passwords discouraged?

2.   Are software scrambling techniques used
        during transmission of vital data?

3.0   <u>SECURITY</u> (Continued)

3.2 <u>Software Security Considerations</u>

3.2.3   <u>Remote Terminals</u>

3.   Are hardware cryptographic devices used during transmission of vital data?

4.   Are terminal users restricted to higher-level languages such as COBOL, FORTRAN, and PL/1, to prevent their access to machine-language coding (which can be used by a knowledgeable systems programmer to override or alter software such as operating systems, security utilities, tables, etc.)?

3.2.4   <u>Operating Systems</u>

1.   Do operating systems have built-in protection to prevent the bypassing of security utilities and the unauthorized access to data bases by a programmer familiar with the system?

2.   Are memory bounds tested following maintenance, initial program load, and restart?

3.   Can software systems technologists be depended upon not to circumvent normal access procedures by use of special coding, thus violating the integrity of the system?

3.2.5   <u>Application Programs</u>

1.   Are well-designed restart and recovery procedures incorporated and utilized?

2.   Do restart procedures properly handle the more complex requirements present by files that are processed in random, rather than sequential, order?

3.   Are programming changes and maintenance controlled and documented?

3.0   <u>SECURITY</u> (Continued)

3.2   <u>Software Security Considerations</u>

3.2.6   <u>Threat Monitoring</u>

1.   Is a monitor log of those who access data banks or sensitive files maintained?

2.   Is there a software routine to monitor attempts to access sensitive files by unauthorized users?

a.   Does this routine notify the operator through the on-line console?

b.   Does this routine provide a record of all such attempts with a printout at day's end?

3.   Does the company use the data obtained above to detect patterns that can help to track down people who misuse or have unauthorized access to vital data records?

4.0   FILES, DOCUMENTATION, AND DATA

4.1   Programs, Libraries, and Control Languages

1. Are duplicate files stored in a building separate from that containing the originals?

2. Is there a current inventory of such files?

3. Have the merits of leasing underground storage space from a reputable vital records concern been considered?

4. Are programs stored in low fire-hazard containers?

5. Has a "dry run" been recently conducted to test the ease and accuracy of the file backup system?

6. Are program changes controlled and recorded?

7. Are changes made only to a copy of a program file, but not to the original?

8. Is a record maintained of items withdrawn from the production file area?

9. Does the computer operations department review systems documentation for compliance with operational standards?

10. Is there a backup of source data for programs under development?

11. Are programs classified according to a predetermined classification policy?

12. Are all computer room and data entry tapes and files retained for at least five days?

13. Are systems, JCL and data entry software tapes stored at a local bank or other safe deposit vault? As major changes are made, are these tapes replaced with updated versions?

14. Are all payroll JCL controlled and accessed only by a minimum of operators?

15. Have data, programs, and documentation been classified in terms of their criticality to the organization?

16. Is there a marking system for evacuating the most critical items first?

4.0   FILES, DOCUMENTATION, AND DATA (Continued)

   4.1 Programs, Libraries, and Control Languages

      17. Are data files of the highest classification kept
           together in racks to permit easy removal?

      18. Is system backup (disk-to-tape-disk) done weekly?
           Is JCL backup (card-to-tape) done monthly?

      19. Is there restricted access to all JCL for
           confidential jobs?

   4.2 Documentation

      4.2.1   Standards

         1. Are there documentation standards that
             include:

             a. Logic or flow charts?

             b. Current listings?

             c. Input and output formats?

             d. Output samples?

             e. User documentation?

             f. Copies of test data?

             g. Adequate explanation of codes,
                 tables, calculations, etc.?

             h. Explanation of error messages?

             i. Rejected record procedures?

             j. Explanation of halts?

             k. File sequence description?

             l. Control and balancing instructions?

      4.2.2   Procedures

         1. Are duplicates of all documentation
             maintained?

         2. Are the duplicates filed in a building
             separate from that containing the
             originals?

47

4.0   FILES, DOCUMENTATION, AND DATA (Continued)

4.2   Documentation

4.2.2   Procedures

3. Are low-fire hazard storage equipment used for documentation?

4. Are the files inventoried at least annually?

5. Is backup documentation reviewed periodically to assure its applicability?

6. Are changes in programs and documentation coordinated and approved by related areas?

7. Are changes reviewed by the internal auditor?

8. Does the computer operations department review systems documentation for compliance with operational standards?

4.3   Data Files

4.3.1   Control Procedures

1. Is the retention cycle for data files documented for each application?

2. Does the user review this procedure regularly for compliance?

3. Are all data files maintained within and under the control of the computer complex rather than the user?

4. Are files classified in terms of degree of sensitivity value to the company?

5. Are the files (tape, disk, or card) kept in an area other than the computer room?

6. Is this area fire protected?

7. Is access to the area specifically controlled?

8. Are special low-fire hazard storage containers used for critical files?

4.3   Data Files

4.3.1   Control Procedures

9.   Is the program for source document retention coordinated with file reconstruction procedures?

10. Is the data file security system tested periodically to assure compliance with standard procedure?

11. Has the relative value of a given program or file been determined?

12. Do appropriate personnel understand the legal requirements for file retention and does the installation comply with those requirements?

13. Does the user participate effectively in a file classification program?

4.3.2   General Procedures

1.   Procedures for removal?

2.   Classification identification?

3.   Ease of equipment removal?

5.0   DISASTER PLANNING CONSIDERATIONS

    5.1 Organization

        1. Does a single individual manage computer security activities?

        2. Has management expressed concern for computer security?

        3. Has a policy for computer security been developed?

        4. To achieve specific goals, is there an effective liaison with in-house service departments, local agencies, or outside consultants in the following areas:

            a. Plant engineering and facilities, construction, electrical, air conditioning, site preparation, etc.?

            b. Plant security (fire protection, watchman, courier services, government requirements, etc.)?

            c. Plant safety?

            d. Vital records management?

            e. Legal staff?

            f. Personnel department (personnel screening, etc.)?

            g. Insurance?

            h. Auditor (system design, policies and procedures, etc.)?

        5. Are functions relating to the control of the organization's assets separated within the organization so that possibility of collusion is minimized?

    5.2 Internal Audit Controls

        1. Is there an overall audit control philosophy relating to computer systems concerned with assets?

        2. Are there controls for computer usage and production?

5.0   <u>DISASTER PLANNING CONSIDERATIONS</u> (Continued)

    5.2   <u>Internal Audit Controls</u>

        3.   Is there control input to assure receipt of all data from the user?

        4.   Is output monitored for compliance with standards?

        5.   Is there an error reporting and follow-up procedure?

        6.   Is there a quality control unit to verify proper execution of a report?

        7.   Are program changes controlled?

        8.   Are all options of all programs tested?

        9.   Are systems conversions controlled so that continuity is assured?

      10.   Are duties (e.g., ordering, record-keeping, custody) separated?

      11.   Is the installation adequately protected against intrusion?

      12.   Is there backup for programs, files, and hardware?

      13.   Is there adequate insurance protection?

      14.   Are systems auditable?

      15.   Is the auditor (internal or external) involved during the system design phase?

    5.3   <u>Time/Resource Sharing</u>

        1.   Are remote terminals available only to selected individuals?

        2.   Is access to terminals controlled by:

           a.   Locked doors?

           b.   Posted guards?

           c.   Other restraints?

         3.   Does the location of the terminals assure each user's privacy?

5.3   Time/Resource Sharing

4. Does control of portable terminals prevent their theft and misuse?

5. Are "passwords" used to identify a specific terminal and user?

6. Is the password protection system really tamper-proof?

7. Is the interval at which passwords are changed appropriate to the security requirements?

8. Is the password combined with physical keys or access badges?

9. Does the system software restrict a given individual to specific data files only?

10. Do software controls limit the right to add, delete, or modify files?

11. Is access to the "keyword" and "lockword" files restricted?

12. Does the system maintain accurate records of all activity against each data file?

13. Are security-override procedures classified at the highest level and is the use of override closely monitored?

14. Are scramblers or other cryptographic techniques utilized, as appropriate?

15. Is the time-resource sharing security system monitored and reviewed?

16. Is program debugging of the security system closely monitored and controlled?

17. Is there software protection of one-line operating systems or applications programs?

5.0   <u>DISASTER PLANNING CONSIDERATIONS</u> (Continued)

    5.4   <u>Insurance</u>

        5.4.1   <u>Coverage</u>

            1.   Does the insurance program consider the following elements?

                a.   Fire?

                b.   Water damage?

                c.   Blanket crime protection?

                d.   Business interruption?

                e.   Damage to company property?

                f.   Natural disasters?

                g.   Fraud?

                h.   Extra expenses?

                i.   Product warranty?

                j.   Insurance against power failure?

            2.   Is there a specific EDP policy that covers:

                a.   Equipment?

                b.   Media?

                c.   Extra expenses?

                d.   Business interruption?

        5.4.2   Other Costs

            1.   Has the organization identified all the costs that would be incurred in a disaster and adequately insured against such losses, including?

                a.   Replacement of hardware?

                b.   Replacement of critical software?

                c.   Replacement of critical applications programming?

5.0   DISASTER PLANNING CONSIDERATIONS (Continued)

5.4 Insurance

5.4.2   Other Costs

d.   Replacement of physical facilities at their current costs?

e.   Temporary replacement for injured personnel?

f.   Opportunity costs due to business interruption?

g.   Potential for natural disaster?

2.   Has insurance coverage been fully evaluated?

5.5 Contingency Planning

5.5.1   Hardware

1.   Where is the backup?

a.   The same room?

b.   A different room, but same building?

c.   A separate location?

d.   Can it handle the workload?

2.   If not, does the organization have access to another computer?

a.   Is there a contractual agreement?

b.   Is the computer tested at least quarterly?

c.   Do installation personnel take computer security seriously?

d.   Can it handle the workload?

3.   Is there an implementation plan for use of a backup installation and is it tested and reviewed periodically?

    5.5   Contingency Planning

        5.5.1   Hardware

            4.   Is there a regular maintenance scheduled, and is it followed?

            5.   Does the vendor stock parts locally?

        5.5.2   Procedures

            1.   Is there a written contingency plan covering:

                a.   Personnel responsible for each functional area?

                b.   A detailed notification procedure clearly specifying the people to be notified and by whom they are to be notified?

                    (1)   Management?
                    (2)   Emergency crews?
                    (3)   Users?
                    (4)   Backup sites?
                    (5)   Service personnel?
                    (6)   Facilities personnel?

                c.   The criteria for determining the extent of disruption?

                d.   The responsibility for retaining source documents and/or data files for each application?

                e.   Identification of backup installation?

                f.   Other considerations, such as:

                    (1)   Purchase or lease of new or temporary equipment?

                    (2)   Acquisition of air conditioning equipment?

                    (3)   Purchase of computer time and service?

DISASTER PLANNING CONSIDERATIONS (Continued)

5.5 Contingency Planning

5.5.2 Procedures

(4) Acquisition of additional manpower?

(5) Acquisition of furnishings, cabinets, etc.?

(6) Acquisition of replacement tapes and disk packs?

(7) Alternate site preparation?

(8) Travel accommodations?

(9) Orderly transportation of computer jobs, personnel and related material?

(10) Duplication of backup files?

(11) Continuing security in contingency mode?

g. Is there a contingency program for all EDP personnel?

2. Are a portion of data processing supplies (cards, forms, etc.) relocated to another area? (Volume should be based upon lead time for new delivery.)

3. Are data processing forms supplied by two vendors?

4. Have all materials needed for disaster plan been located and stored?

5. Is there an emergency call list? Computer operations and programming personnel should each have phone numbers and alternate phone numbers for:

a. Department personnel

b. Vendors -- office and home

c. Management

DISASTER PLANNING CONSIDERATIONS (Continued)

5.5 Contingency Planning

5.5.2 Procedures

6. Have arrangements been made with suppliers for the speedy replacement of:

    a. Forms and card stock?

    b. Magnetic storage media?

    c. Air conditioning equipment?

    d. Electrical equipment?

    e. Detection and prevention equipment?

    f. Security equipment?

    g. Construction materials?

        (1) Flooring?
        (2) Ceiling?
        (3) Partitioning?
        (4) Other related materials?

    h. Computing equipment?

    i. Data entry devices?

    j. Communications equipment?

7. Have arrangements been made for freight capabilities for such replacement and to move backup equipment, files, documents, etc.?

8. Have arrangements been made for specialized repair and/or cleanup services?

9. Is there an annual service contract with a qualified fire and security systems maintenance service organization?

5.5   Contingency Planning

5.5.2   Procedures

10. Has the appointment of a "security task force" been considered to:

  a.   Perform random inspections?

  b.   Perform random audits?

  c.   Verify the use of protection procedures?

  d.   Verify the currentness and protection of both programs and data?

  e.   Verify the disaster prevention techniques?

  f.   Call and monitor disaster training exercise?

5.6   Disaster

5.6.1   Prevention

1. Has a disaster team been designated?

2. Have procedures been established for the sequence of events to be followed during and after a disaster?

3. Has a master plan been established for disaster contingencies? Is the plan kept current?

4. What personnel notification procedures exist?

5. Are all team members provided with copies of home or other telephone numbers to notify team members or other department members?

6. Has a notification procedure been established?

7. Would it be useful to develop a pyramid structure notification procedure?

5.6   Disaster

5.6.1   Prevention

8. Is there an alternate plan for notification if the telephone system is nonfunctional (as in the case of a natural disaster)?

9. Have established procedures been tested to determine if they work and then modified, if necessary?

10. Do notification procedures establish precisely:

a. Whom each person is to call?

b. What to do if the notification chain breaks down?

c. What each person is to do externally for the organization?

d. Where each person must report, and to whom?

e. The sequence of events once these people are on-site?

11. How will the user be notified: As part of the pyramid structure, separately, or by a responsible official?

12. How will the responsible company officials be notified?

13. Has an alternate site within the organization complex been located to reestablish the base of operations?

14. If destruction of the facility necessitates an alternate location, has the alternate facility been located?

5.6   Disaster

5.6.1   Prevention

15. In evaluating the alternate facility, are the proper site facilities available or can they be expeditiously arranged?

     a.   Power and lighting?

     b.   Air conditioning?

     c.   Humidity control, where necessary?

     d.   Alternate disaster proceedings, in case of a secondary disaster?

16. Who will be responsible for notification of the news media? Who is the official spokesman for the organization? In what form will the notification take place: press releases, telephone calls, or interviews?

17. Have arrangements been made with the vendor for duplicate or similar hardware to be installed on short notice?

18. How will vendors be notified in case of disaster? Who will contact account representatives, customer engineers, and systems engineers?

19. To begin functioning again:

     a.   Have arrangements been made to install a copy of the current operating system on the backup hardware? Is a copy of the operating system stored in a safe place? Has it been maintained and tested periodically?

     b.   Must communications lines be reestablished? How will the communications services and communications equipment vendors be notified? What will their role be in reestablishing communications facilities?

5.6   Disaster

5.6.1   Prevention

c.   Once the recovery hardware is in place and functioning, is there additional backup to accommodate problems or overflow?

d.   Have steps been taken to duplicate programs and decks so that the organization has the proper disaster protection?

e.   Is a software or other control specialist available to ensure that job control specifications are valid and functioning? Has the job control language been duplicated again to provide backup?

f.   Is there an emergency distribution of forms and supplies? If backup forms and supplies are used, have steps been taken to replenish that supply?

g.   Have steps been taken to duplicate the critical files, library programs, software, etc., necessary to reestablish backup?

h.   Have operator run books or documentation been duplicated for backup?

20.   What priority scheme is established for recovery? What runs will be done first to get the company functioning again? If it is not part of the disaster plan, who will make the decision during recovery?

21.   What personnel realignments, additions, etc., will be necessary during the recovery period?

22.   Must specialized support services be used during this period?

a.   Commercially available payroll services?

5.6   Disaster

5.6.1   Prevention

b.   Commercially available time-sharing?

c.   Use of specialized consulting services during the period?

d.   Specialized and short term for new personnel?

e.   Commercially available distribution services, such as mail trucks, courier services, security services?

23.   Can additional tapes, disks, etc., be obtained on short notice? Have arrangements been made for replenishing media?

24.   Can temporary furniture, equipment racks, storage for cards, tapes, disks, etc., be obtained on short notice?

25.   Can office supplies and equipment be obtained on short notice?

26.   Have the organization's legal representatives been contacted to determine liability for data, services, equipment, etc.?

27.   Have the organization's insurance representatives been contacted to determine coverages, liabilities, and to arrange for coverage for the new site?

28.   Has the accounting department been contacted to determine what manual records exist to assist in reconstructing data records? Could the accounting department assume any manual backup operations during the interim period, so that critical receivables can be obtained, processed, and accounted for; payroll services can be maintained; and accounts payable systems can be continued to receive trade discounts?

5.6   Disaster

5.6.1   Prevention

29.   Have other departments requiring data processing information been contacted with similar requests?

30.   Have real estate representatives been contacted to determine the availability of reconstruction sites if the organization will not rebuild on the destroyed site?

31.   Has all written documentation been obtained and duplicated and has the copy been stored safely?

32.   Have supervisory personnel been assigned to ensure that manual or backup systems are functioning properly during the interim period?

33.   Has responsibility for cleanup of the destroyed site been assigned, or has that service been otherwise obtained?

34.   Have contacts been established for reconstruction or refurbishing of the data center, to include electrical, air conditioning, humidity control, fire prevention, heating, security, etc.?

35.   Have short-range and long-range planning begun to return the installation to normalcy?

36.   Have public relations tasks been performed?

5.6.2   Recovery

1.   If a computer service bureau is to be used, have the following items been considered?

a.   Is its location in a low-risk area?

b.   Does it control access to their computer and file areas?

5.0   <u>DISASTER PLANNING CONSIDERATIONS</u> (Continued)

   5.6   <u>Disaster</u>

      5.6.2   <u>Recovery</u>

            c.   Is its customer work area secure?

            d.   Is its fire or other danger
                  potential low?

            e.   Does its housekeeping program
                  enhance the security of data?

            f.   Will it handle an organization's
                  work with consideration of its
                  value?

            g.   Is its personnel competent and
                  concerned?

            h.   Are its couriers efficient and
                  trustworthy?

            i.   Does it screen all of its employees?

            j.   Are its operating and control
                  procedures adequate?

            k.   Does the contract permit the
                  organization to recover any loss
                  due to:

                  (1)   Erroneous results?
                  (2)   Inadvertent release of data?
                  (3)   Loss of vital files?

            l.   Is it in a position to pay if it is
                  liable for a loss?

                  (1)   Is it insured for liability?
                  (2)   Is it financially sound?
                  (3)   What are its financial
                        affiliations?

            m.   Does the organization know the loss
                  potential of the work it is
                  processing?

PILOT BOOKS READING SHELF

CHECKLIST/GUIDE TO SELECTING A SMALL COMPUTER by Wilma E. Bennett
Avoid making the mistake of selecting the wrong type of computer. Proper equipment increases productivity and improves management decisions. The book contains a checklist of 332 questions enabling you to compare equipment from different sources and then decide which unit is best for you. Includes a glossary of 163 computer terms and abbreviations, defined in everyday English to cut through unnecessary jargon.   **$5.00**

PREPARING EFFECTIVE PRESENTATIONS by Ray J. Friant, Jr.
How to develop presentations that pay-off. The author originally developed this simplified procedure for use by General Electric and it is still being used by them. The book shows that the preparation of an effective presentation is not complicated, difficult or time consuming. The material covered is stripped of time consuming and wasteful verbiage. The book offers a simple methodology for presenting complicated ideas to diverse audiences. It shows both the experienced and inexperienced how to prevent errors in constructing and offering presentations.   **$3.50**

THE EXECUTIVE'S GUIDE TO HANDLING A PRESS INTERVIEW by Dick Martin
Written by an executive of one of the country's leading industrial firms who has helped hundreds of executives to prepare for press interviews. This book offers specific techniques to use in dealing with the press, even in the face of hostility, criticism and attack. Get the assurance you need to be more responsive and to get your story across. Also covers phone, radio, television and news conferences.   **$3.95**

HOW TO HANDLE SPEECHWRITING ASSIGNMENTS, by Douglas P. Starr
Provides a guide for the person who must write a speech for someone else. The speech may have to be written for business, political, government, military or public relations purposes. This book presents formulas and techniques that show how to write an informative, meaningful, and successful speech and tailor it to the speaker's own personality.   **$3.95**

PREPARING CONTRACT-WINNING PROPOSALS AND FEASIBILITY STUDIES by Tim Whalen
Written by an award-winning specialist, this manual covers the entire process. The methodology can easily be tailored to the requirements of your business and the special needs of a particular Request for Proposal. This system, when carefully followed, increases the success rate of the proposal and feasibility study process. **$5.00**

Pilot Books   103 Cooper Street, Babylon, New York 11702